WHAT MAKES A VAN GOGH
A VAN GOGH?

Richard Mühlberger

The Metropolitan Museum of Art

CHERRYTREE BOOKS

A Cherrytree Book
First published in 1993 by The Metropolitan Museum of Art, New York, and
Viking, a division of Penguin Books USA Inc.
Copyright © 1993 by The Metropolitan Museum of Art
What Makes a . . . a . . . ? is a trademark of The Metropolitan Museum of Art.

This edition first published in 1994 by Cherrytree Press Ltd, Windsor Bridge
Road, Bath, Avon BA2 3AX.
Copyright © Cherrytree Press Ltd, 1994.

Produced by the Department of Special Publications
The Metropolitan Museum of Art
Series Editor: Mary Beth Brewer
Front Cover Design: Marleen Adlerblum
Design: Nai Y. Chang
Printing and Binding: A. Mondadori, Verona, Italy

British Library Cataloguing in Publication Data
Mühlberger, Richard
    What Makes a Van Gogh a Van Gogh?
    I. Title
    759.9493

ISBN 0-7451-5252-X Hardcover
ISBN 0-7451-5230-9 Softcover

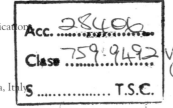
ILLUSTRATIONS
Unless otherwise noted, all works are by Vincent van Gogh and in oil on canvas.

Pages 1 and 2: *Cypresses*, 93 × 74 cm (36³/₄ × 29¹/₈ in.), 1889, The Metropolitan Museum of Art, Rogers Fund, 1949, 49.30; photograph, Malcolm Varon.

Page 6: photograph, Vincent van Gogh, 1866, Vincent van Gogh Foundation/Van Gogh Museum, Amsterdam.

Page 8: *Hand with Bowl and Cat*, black chalk, 20 × 33 cm (7⁷/₈ × 13 in.), Vincent van Gogh Foundation/Van Gogh Museum, Amsterdam.

Page 9: *The Potato Peeler*, 40 × 32 cm (16 × 12¹/₂ in.), 1885, The Metropolitan Museum of Art, Bequest of Miss Adelaide Milton de Groot (1876-1967), 1967, 67.187.70b; photograph, Malcolm Varon.

Page 9: *Peasant Woman Cooking by a Fireplace*, 44 × 38 cm (17³/₈ × 15 in.), 1885, The Metropolitan Museum of Art, Gift of Mr. and Mrs. Mortimer Hays, 1984, 1984.393.

Page 11: *The Potato Eaters*, 82 × 114 cm (32¹/₄ × 44⁷/₈ in.), Vincent van Gogh Foundation/ Van Gogh Museum, Amsterdam.

Page 12: Paul Signac, *The Jetty at Cassis*, 46 × 65 cm (18¹/₄ × 25⁵/₈ in.), 1889, The Metropolitan Museum of Art, Bequest of Joan Whitney Payson, 1975, 1976.201.19; photograph, Malcolm Varon.

Page 13: *Self-Portrait in Front of an Easel*, 65 × 51 cm (25⁵/₈ × 20¹/₈ in.), Vincent van Gogh Foundation/Van Gogh Museum, Amsterdam.

Page 13: *Self-Portrait with Grey Felt Hat*, 44 × 38 cm (17³/₈ × 15 in.), Vincent van Gogh Foundation/Van Gogh Museum, Amsterdam.

Page 15: *Portrait of Père Tanguy*, 65 × 51 cm (25⁵/₈ × 20¹/₈ in.), Hôtel de Chanaleilles, Paris; photograph, Scala/Art Resource, New York.

Page 16: *Vincent's House*, 76 × 94 cm (29⁷/₈ × 37 in.), 1888, Vincent van Gogh Foundation/ Van Gogh Museum, Amsterdam.

Page 17: *Sunflowers*, 43 × 61 cm (17 × 24 in.), 1887, The Metropolitan Museum of Art, Rogers Fund, 1949, 49.41.

Page 19: *Sunflowers*, 93 × 73 cm (36⁵/₈ × 28³/₄ in.), reproduced by courtesy of the Trustees, The National Gallery, London.

Page 21: *The Café Terrace at Night, 'Place du Forum,' Arles*, 81 × 66 cm (31⁷/₈ × 26 in.), Collection: State Museum Kröller-Müller, Otterlo, The Netherlands.

Page 22: Jacob van Ruisdael, *Wheatfields*, 100 × 130 cm (39³/₈ × 51¹/₄ in.), The Metropolitan Museum of Art, Bequest of Benjamin Altman, 1913, 14.40.623.

Page 23: *Harvest at La Crau*, 73 × 92 cm (28³/₄ × 36¹/₄ in.), Vincent van Gogh Foundation/ Van Gogh Museum, Amsterdam.

Page 24: *The Blue Cart*, graphite, black chalk, oil pastel (?), brown ink, watercolour and gouache on tan paper, 39 × 52 cm (15¹/₂ × 20⁵/₈ in.), 1888, Courtesy of The Fogg Art Museum, Harvard University Art Museums, Bequest of Grenville L. Winthrop.

Page 26: *The Bedroom*, 74 × 92 cm (29 × 36¹/₈ in.), 1888, Helen Birch Bartlett Memorial Collection, 1926.417; photograph ©1992 The Art Institute of Chicago. All Rights Reserved.

Page 28: *Gauguin's Chair*, 96 × 72 cm (37⁵/₈ × 28³/₈ in.), Vincent van Gogh Foundation/Van Gogh Museum, Amsterdam.

Page 29: *Van Gogh's Chair (The Chair and the Pipe)*, 93 × 74 cm (36⁵/₈ × 29¹/₈ in.), reproduced by courtesy of the Trustees, The National Gallery, London.

Page 31: *L'Arlésienne: Madame Joseph-Michel Ginoux (Marie Julien, 1848-1911)*, 91 × 74 cm (36 × 29 in.), 1888, The Metropolitan Museum of Art, Bequest of Sam A. Lewisohn, 1951, 51.112.3; photograph, Malcolm Varon.

Page 33: *Cypresses*, 93 × 74 cm (36³/₄ × 29¹/₈ in.), 1889, The Metropolitan Museum of Art, Rogers Fund, 1949, 49.30; photograph, Malcolm Varon.

Page 34: *Cypresses*, reed pen and bistre, 62 × 46 cm (24¹/₂ × 18 in.), 1889, The Brooklyn Museum, Frank L. Babbott and A. Augustus Healy Fund, 38.123.19.

Page 35: *Wheatfield*, 24 × 32 cm (9¹/₂ × 12¹/₂ in.), pen, reed pen, and brown ink over pencil, The Metropolitan Museum of Art, Gift of Mrs. Max J. H. Rossbach, 1964, 64.125.3.

Page 36: *The Starry Night*, 74 × 92 cm (29 × 36¹/₄ in.), 1889, Collection, The Museum of Modern Art, New York, Acquired through the Lillie P. Bliss Bequest.

Page 40: Jean-François Millet, *First Steps*, black chalk with squaring by van Gogh, Vincent van Gogh Foundation/Van Gogh Museum, Amsterdam.

Page 42: *First Steps, after Millet*, 72 × 91 cm (28¹/₂ × 35⁷/₈ in.), 1890, The Metropolitan Museum of Art, Gift of George N. and Helen M. Richard, 1964, 64.165.2; photograph, Malcolm Varon.

Pages 44-45: *Crows over a Wheatfield*, 51 × 101 cm (20¹/₈ × 39³/₄ in.), Vincent van Gogh Foundation/Van Gogh Museum, Amsterdam.

Page 47: *Irises*, 74 × 92 cm (29 × 36¹/₄ in.), 1890, The Metropolitan Museum of Art, Gift of Adele R. Levy, 1958, 58.187; photograph, Malcolm Varon.

Page 49: *The Bank of the Oise at Auvers*, 73 × 94 cm (28³/₄ × 37 in.), 1890, © The Detroit Institute of Arts, Bequest of Robert H. Tannahill.

CONTENTS

At boarding school thirteen-year-old Vincent was not sociable. His sister wrote that
he had a head of reddish hair and eyes that were blue or green 'according to his changing expressions'. His brow, she reported, 'was already slightly wrinkled, his eyebrows
drawn together in deep thought'.

Meet Vincent van Gogh

Vincent Willem van Gogh was born on 30 March 1853, in the Dutch village of Groot-Zundert, near the Belgian border. His father, the son of a minister, was a minister himself. From his father's side of the family, Vincent inherited a deep respect for humanity, while his mother passed on to him her love of art and nature. Pastor and Mrs van Gogh made great sacrifices to send their three daughters and three sons to good schools. Vincent, the oldest, was the first to go away to school. He was eleven at the time and was sad to leave home. He was an average student but worked very hard, and by the age of thirteen was studying Dutch, German, French and English, as well as arithmetic, history, geography, botany, zoology, calligraphy and gymnastics. He also took drawing lessons. But in March 1868, Vincent abruptly returned home and spent a year with his parents and then decided not to finish school. He was sixteen years old when he left home to earn a living.

His first job was in an art gallery. Next he became a schoolteacher, and then, following in his father's footsteps, he became a minister. He chose to work in a desperately poor mining district, where he suffered great poverty but found solace in making drawings of the miners. After about two years, Vincent was convinced that he was meant to serve humanity through art. From that moment, he never stopped drawing and painting.

During his short life, van Gogh earned almost no money at all and depended on an allowance that his brother Theo sent him. Vincent wrote many letters to Theo, whom he loved deeply, and it is from them that so much is known of Vincent's life and art.

This book begins in 1885, when van Gogh painted his first large canvas, a personal triumph after almost five years of continuous study and practice. It shows the unusual subject of a peasant family eating potatoes. Van Gogh wrote to his brother that what he tried most was 'to bring life into it'. As this book follows van Gogh's brief journey, you will see that his remarkable style brought life into everything he painted.

The Potato Eaters

Van Gogh's First Masterpiece

Vincent van Gogh was thirty-two years old when he painted his first masterpiece. In preparation for the painting, he had spent an entire winter drawing pictures and painting small studies of the stolid, hardworking peasants of the poor region where he lived. Van Gogh wrote to his brother Theo, 'By witnessing peasant life continually, at all hours of the day, I have become so absorbed in it that I hardly ever think of anything else.' Van Gogh became friendly with one peasant family, the De Groots. In their grimy, thatched cottage, van Gogh was inspired to try to paint a picture larger and more important than any he had done before.

The magical way the flickering flame of a lamp illuminated the dark interior of the De Groots' cottage fascinated van Gogh. The flame made objects and people visible in the darkness, something he would attempt with paint. While van Gogh studied the dim light from the flame, he also saw how his friends lived. He decided that his painting would show the entire De Groot family around a table under the lamp, with a dish of steaming potatoes before them.

To memorize how the De Groots looked and acted, van Gogh made dozens of paintings and sketches of their heads and hands. The De Groots were patient with their artist friend, and all winter long, allowed him to make oil studies of them by day whenever he found them not working, and drawings by night. Finally, he felt he could paint them from memory.

Earth Colours and Colourful White

Describing one of his oil studies, van Gogh said it was 'painted with earth'. That was the feeling it had. As a matter of fact, some of the pigments that he used are called earth colours because they come from clay, rocks and mineral deposits. Van Gogh had studied seventeenth-century Dutch paintings, in which dark, earthy colours with touches of white were often used. He wanted his paintings to look like them.

Actually, most of the white seen in *The Potato Eaters* is not white at all. Pure white would

HAND WITH BOWL AND CAT

8

have been too bright in the dark room. It is a light grey that looks like white because it is lighter than any other colour in the painting. Only to paint highlights did van Gogh use small touches of pure white.

Making People Larger Than Life
Van Gogh painted *The Potato Eaters* in a small bedroom that he rented as a studio from the caretaker of the local Catholic church; he slept in an even smaller space in the attic. His studio was almost as dark as the room in the painting. When he was unsure of a detail as he worked, he would tuck the canvas under his arm and hurry to the De Groots' cottage.

The De Groots' arms and legs look longer in

THE POTATO PEELER

PEASANT WOMAN COOKING BY A FIREPLACE

the painting than they were in real life; if the painted family all stood up, they would be noble giants. Van Gogh extended their limbs to give these kind peasants greater importance, just as artists of old did with figures of saints. Van Gogh also exaggerated their facial features to emphasize their inner strength. These stalwart farmers communicate care and affection for one another without speaking.

Simple Pleasures

Potatoes must have been boring for the De Groots, since they ate them every day. But they surely looked forward to sipping the freshly brewed coffee that is here poured with simple ceremony. Van Gogh shows how much they appreciate the drink by picturing one of the men eagerly holding up his cup and the second man looking up from the potatoes to the aromatic treat across the table. The potatoes may represent the earthbound monotony of peasant life, but the coffee represents its simple pleasures.

As van Gogh worked on his masterpiece, he became more interested in the De Groots than in the flame of the lamp. He shrouded unnecessary details in shadows so that each face seems as much a light in the dark room as the lamp is. This was van Gogh's way of showing the dignity of these farmers whom he so greatly respected.

With growing confidence in himself, van Gogh left Holland to study painting in Antwerp, Belgium, where he learned to use brighter colours.

But after three months there, he was still a Dutch painter of solid facts. What now interested him were the aims of a group of young painters in Paris who captured the fleeting impressions of light. His brother Theo lived in Paris and was friendly with many of these new artists, so Vincent decided to join him and moved to Paris in 1886.

Soon after van Gogh painted the De Groot family, he wrote, 'I like so much better to paint the eyes of people than to paint cathedrals.' The eyes were generally regarded as windows to the soul; to van Gogh, a painting of a face was as spiritual as a painting of a church.

THE POTATO EATERS

The Potato Eaters *was van Gogh's driving interest from early April until*
6 May 1885, when he completed it. He never spent so many days on a picture
again, but this was his first important work, and he wanted to make a big
impression with it.

11

Self-Portrait with Grey Felt Hat

Painting with Dots and Dashes of Colour

In Paris, van Gogh painted more than twenty self-portraits, and in only two early ones did he feature the earth colours of his native Holland. After he met a young artist named Paul Signac, van Gogh filled the backgrounds of his self-portraits with lively colours and patterns.

Signac was ten years younger than van Gogh, but this did not stop them from becoming friends and going to the country together on painting excursions. Signac had learned a new method of painting that was to become known as pointillism. In pointillism small dots, or points, of unmixed colour were dabbed on to the canvas next to one another so they would appear to blend when a viewer stepped back from the painting.

Deciding on the colour of each dot required some knowledge of colour theory, and van Gogh had no time for mixing science and art. But when he saw the beautiful paintings that resulted from pointillism, he adopted the method Signac taught him. Even with Signac coaching him, though, van Gogh would not paint an entire canvas with dots. Signac kept trying to get him to do it; van Gogh kept making his dots into dashes. But to make his young friend feel better, van Gogh painted sleeves of a blue work shirt with little dots of colour and wore it when he went painting with Signac.

Painting the Modern Way

In *Self-Portrait in Front of an Easel*, painted early in 1888 and one of van Gogh's last Parisian self-portraits, the artist remembered what Signac taught him but added much more from his own imagination. Here, he even depicts his palette with short dashes of colour on it. In *Self-Portrait with Grey Felt Hat*, the dabs and dashes of colour follow the curving surfaces of van Gogh's face and shoulders, as well as the outline of his head and upper body. As Signac promised van Gogh, from a distance the dabs and dashes blend into colours that look like the actual colours of the things he painted — van Gogh's face, hair, clothing and hat. Close to, the effect is more like a mask.

Paul Signac
THE JETTY AT CASSIS

Paul Signac's enthusiasm for painting with small dots of colour awakened van Gogh's appreciation for modern ways of expressing himself. He preferred bigger and bolder patterns, but enjoyed experimenting with the method his young friend used in paintings like this one.

SELF-PORTRAIT IN FRONT OF AN EASEL

Although he cast a shadow across almost his entire face, van Gogh painted his beard so it seems to glow from within by putting orange and blue near each other. This contrast emphasizes both colours, just as the squared corners of the stretched canvas and palette bring out the curves of the head and shoulders.

SELF-PORTRAIT WITH GREY FELT HAT

The patterns of short, colourful lines radiating from his eyes and circling his head are done in van Gogh's very own new style. He eventually devised other ways to paint portraits, reserving broken patterns for landscapes, but for the moment, this self-portrait proved that he had become a modern artist at last.

Portrait of Père Tanguy

When van Gogh first arrived in Paris, he knew no one but his brother, but that was to change quickly. On his second day in the city, van Gogh met Julien Tanguy, who had an art-supply shop midway between Theo's art gallery and the flat the two van Gogh brothers shared. Artists found Julien Tanguy kind and generous, and they affectionately called him Père ('father') Tanguy.

It was at Père Tanguy's cramped shop that van Gogh had met Paul Signac and many other artists. The shop was a place to learn new ideas. Tanguy liked art that was not traditional, and he sold paintings that were different and unusual. Van Gogh decided to honour Tanguy by painting his portrait. He showed the kind man with his hands folded on his lap, his glasses neatly tucked into his jacket pocket. Behind him, the wall is papered with Japanese prints.

When van Gogh painted the portrait, he had been collecting Japanese prints for two years. Eventually he owned hundreds like the ones that cover the wall behind Père Tanguy. Tanguy himself apparently did not collect these exotic works of art, nor did he sell them in his shop; perhaps they are behind him in the portrait simply to express his great love of art. They also serve as a lively contrast to this solid shopkeeper.

Tanguy is posed exactly in the centre of the canvas, his left side almost perfectly balancing his right side. Above him is a print of Japan's famous Mount Fuji. The neckline of Tanguy's coat and its lapels are three V shapes, each like the sacred mountain. The angle between his legs also repeats the shape of Fuji. The other prints behind him do not echo his pose; instead, they show flowers, people and a landscape, subjects that van Gogh loved to paint.

Van Gogh's Hobby

Japan became van Gogh's hobby. He read everything he could get his hands on about the country and its art, and was convinced that Japan's was the ideal society. To bring himself closer to the great artists of Japan, he made careful, painted copies of a few of the most dramatic Japanese prints he could find.

The prints behind Père Tanguy were cheaply made in Japan and came to Paris as packing material in crates of merchandise. Once Parisian artists saw their bold colours, strong outlines and unusual perspectives, they wanted to copy them in their own pictures. Before long, the throwaway prints were being collected.

Sunflowers

On to Arles

It was the coldest month of 1888 when van Gogh left Paris for the south of France, where the sun was brighter and where he hoped to find warmer days and clearer skies. The artist's destination, the ancient town of Arles, became his home for almost fifteen months. While he was there, he enjoyed the most productive period of his life, painting nearly two hundred canvases and making more than a hundred drawings and watercolours. 'I go on like a painting locomotive,' he said, describing his fervent activity.

When he arrived in Arles, van Gogh knew no one, but he liked the place well enough to search for a house where he could live and paint. After a few months, he rented one he could afford on the outskirts of town near the railway station, and he lived in various hotels while painting and furnishing his new home. Van Gogh's house was opposite a public garden where oleanders grew. Sunflowers edged the railway line and golden fields of wheat stretched to low-lying hills in the distance, inviting the artist to walk and to paint.

Golden Flowers

In his letters to Theo, van Gogh commented enthusiastically on how beautifully nature combines the blue of the sky with the yellow of the fields. He envisaged six paintings of sunflowers to decorate his house, describing them as 'a symphony in blue and yellow'. The 'raw chrome yellows [of the sunflowers] will blaze forth' against the blues, he wrote.

VINCENT'S HOUSE

In making this picture of his new surroundings in Arles, van Gogh painted his little four-room house against the bluest of skies. He knew the colours would intensify one another.

OPPOSITE:
SUNFLOWERS

Van Gogh first found sunflowers on the edge of Paris, where city and country met, and he painted this detailed view of them. The spiky dried petals, each reaching out separately, contrast with the evenly packed centre of seeds.

Cut sunflowers wilt quickly, so van Gogh rose at dawn to gather enough flowers for a painting, and then would 'do the whole in one rush'. The rest of the day, he painted other subjects. He wanted to finish enough sunflower paintings to brighten the guest room and studio of his house in time for a visit by Paul Gauguin, an artist friend whom van Gogh greatly admired. He completed at least four sunflower paintings by the time Gauguin arrived. His guest loved them, and even made a portrait of van Gogh painting a canvas filled with the yellow flowers.

Painting Light on Light

In this painting of sunflowers, a thin blue line separates the dark table from the pale wall and enlivens the yellow tones. There is also a blue line around the belly of the vase that serves as a border between the areas of dark and pale yellow. Van Gogh added touches of blue to the bottom and left side of the vase, too. In painting golden flowers against a yellow background, van Gogh said he was dealing with 'light on light'. To van Gogh, yellow represented the sun.

Energy and Motion

In van Gogh's exuberant depiction of them, the fifteen sunflowers take on individual personalities. Each one is a slightly different size, and some are laden with petals while others are losing them. The six fattest flowers, down the centre of the picture, are formed by clusters of small, thick dabs of dark orange paint, making them look like seed balls almost ready to burst. The other sunflowers extend orange and green tendrils. These curled and jagged lines appear to be in constant wavelike motion, filling the spaces between blossoms and animating them.

The vase is divided into two sections, contrasting with the two colours of the background. The top is brightly coloured, so it stands out against the yellow wall. The bottom is pale yellow, making it stand out against the dark tabletop. In proper Japanese style, nothing in the painting casts a shadow. This makes the bottom of the vase look as flat as the wall behind it.

Sunflowers is as much a symbolic painting as it is a celebration of nature's bounty. Almost two years after he painted the sunflower series, in a letter to his sister Willemien, van Gogh said that the flowers 'may symbolize gratitude'. At the time he painted them, his heart was full of thanks to his brother for his support, to Gauguin for his friendship, and to the sun for its light and warmth.

Van Gogh's dream to decorate his house entirely with sunflower paintings might seem too much of a good thing, but his scheme was to vary each painting. Backgrounds would be yellow or blue, combinations he believed would provide endless visual stimulation. After a few were painted, he decided yellow against yellow looked best, and he stuck to this scheme.

The Café Terrace at Night

A Friendly Café

Cafés are usually lively, sociable places, and they were beloved by the artists of the nineteenth century. As the word café indicates, coffee was served there, as well as other drinks and light meals. For the artists in van Gogh's day, conversation was the main course, provided by the loyal clientele. (Some went so regularly that their mail was delivered there.) Van Gogh knew of a stylish café in the centre of Arles where people enjoyed the warm evenings outdoors, and he went there to paint this picture.

In the painting, van Gogh created three kinds of light. A gas lamp reaches out from the café wall on a bracket and emits an intense yellow radiance. The underside of the awning bounces its reflection back to the tabletops and out on to the street. A second, softer light comes from the windows and doors. To create this light, van Gogh scattered patches of orange throughout the canvas. The largest of these are the windows and doors of the café itself and of the corner shop across the street. The third kind of light comes from the stars in the heavens, some of which van Gogh painted with strokes of luminous silver to suggest the way real stars shine. The tables on the terrace below almost seem to be their reflections.

The Richly Coloured Night

Small figures under the awning are silhouetted against areas of lively colour. The diagonal lines made by the ruts in the cobblestones, the edges of the awning, the orange terrace, and the slant of the doors and window in the café wall all lead to them. A man enters the café. A waiter is ready to take an order. Customers sit beneath the dazzling light from the gas lamp as it makes the colours of the walls and the street glow. In the walls, yellow shifts to orange and green. The pavement stones are lavender, purple, blue, yellow, orange and even a little pink. 'The night is more alive and more richly coloured than the day,' van Gogh wrote to Theo. He was proud of painting 'a night picture without any black, nothing but beautiful blue and violet and green'. His enthusiasm for the colours shows in the generous way he applied them. Even in a reproduction of this painting, his thick brushstrokes are apparent across the underside of the awning and in the deep green pine branches opposite it.

Although it is late at night in the town van Gogh used bright colours to depict the café terrace. The darkest areas are made up of deep blue, green and purple. Nowhere can pure black be found. His artist friends in Paris taught him that even shadows are composed of a mixture of colours.

Harvest at La Crau

A Sea of Fields

In June and July of 1888, van Gogh took many walks into the countryside around Arles. He told his sister that he looked like a dusty porcupine on these excursions, with his easel, canvases, paints, 'and other merchandise' bristling out from across his shoulders and back, under his arms, and dangling from both hands. La Crau is three miles northeast of Arles, and van Gogh made about fifty outings there, painting and drawing the fields and farm buildings. Although *Harvest at La Crau* looks tranquil, van Gogh was fighting strong, steady winds as he painted it. 'The canvas was shaking all the time,' he wrote. There were also biting mosquitoes. 'If a view makes you forget these annoyances, it must have something in it,' he stated.

Van Gogh found the fields of La Crau to be 'as beautiful and as infinite as the sea'. He wanted to memorize the landscape, for he had something special in mind. He did not want to picture it from ground level, for that would prevent him from showing how the fields seem to go on endlessly. He wanted the same sense of infinity as is captured in the sweeping landscape vistas painted by the seventeenth-century Dutch artist Jacob van Ruisdael. In van Ruisdael's paintings, scenes were viewed from on high. Having studied the landscape from ground level, van Gogh imagined it from an elevated vantage point and painted it that way. The high perspective made the fields seem to go on much farther than van Gogh could actually see as he wandered through them.

The Blue Cart

Van Gogh wanted to lead the viewer's eye quickly from the foreground of the painting to the background. He did this by careful planning. Long strokes of the brush at the bottom of the

Jacob van Ruisdael
WHEATFIELDS

THE BLUE CART (DRAWING)

canvas rush the eye to two small fields. On the edge of these plots of land, a blue cart commands the very centre of the painting. Its long wooden shafts and the fence beside it direct the eye back and forth across the canvas before allowing the viewer to explore the green and yellow fields beyond. Van Gogh bordered the fields with lines that quickly lead to the abandoned monastery and to the low mountains in the distance. At the end of that summer, van Gogh decided that this painting was the best thing he had done.

Van Gogh created textures with his Japanese pen that he did not attempt to imitate with his paintbrush. The painting shows the variety of vegetation through different colours, while a drawing of the same subject uses dots, dashes, squiggles and different patterns of parallel lines.

The Bedroom

A House and Bedroom of his Own

When van Gogh could afford to furnish his house, he selected simple furniture for his bedroom and more fancy pieces for the guest room. The four-room house was a home of his own, the only one he ever had. Gauguin was coming to visit, and van Gogh dreamed that other artists would soon flood to Arles. His home would be 'the studio of the south'. In addition to the sunflower paintings, he planned to hang other works so Gauguin could see them. A painting of his bedroom would be among them.

Van Gogh approached the project with zest. He made two drawings of the room, and 'thought out loud' in a long letter to Theo about the colours he would use which he felt should suggest sleep and 'rest the brain'. When he finished the painting, it pleased him so much that he made a copy of it for his sister Willemien and his mother.

Jarring Colours and Outlines

Van Gogh confessed that it was not easy 'to achieve simplicity with garish colours'. One way he did this was by using large areas of flat colours — blue, green, yellow, lavender and red. These jarring hues made familiar things stand out. He had other ways of doing this as well. Every piece of furniture is outlined in black or dark brown for emphasis. By not using shadows under them, van Gogh made the objects appear flat, just as things looked in Japanese prints. The pieces almost seem to float above the floor. He sloped the floor itself so that the right side is higher than the left, and the rear wall slants back from the bed. All this makes for a somewhat topsy-turvy place; only the furniture looks stable. In contrast to the room, the furniture has 'a familiar and reassuring spirit' that van Gogh said makes repose possible.

Empty Chairs and Other Symbols

The little nightstand is tidily set up for van Gogh's use. There is soap in a dish, a pitcher and glass for drinking water, another pitcher and bowl for washing, two bottles and a hairbrush. The brightest spot in the painting is the mirror above the nightstand. A dash of white makes it stand out against the wall. A coarse linen towel with a narrow red inner border hangs from a nail next to the door. The two chairs, their rush seats slanting as the floor does, and the two fluffy pillows on the bed might be symbols of van Gogh's constant wish for someone to share his life.

Interior views were a Dutch tradition in which an artist showed off his knowledge of perspective in painting the floorboards and walls. Van Gogh invented his own system of perspective to make his bedroom inviting. Instead of leading the eye back to the far wall, van Gogh's floor seems to pause at each piece of furniture.

27

For hundreds of years, Western artists have used symbols based on Greek, Roman and Christian traditions. Van Gogh's symbols were more personal, emerging from his deepest thoughts and hopes. As a student away from home, he wept at the sight of an empty chair used by his father during a visit. To van Gogh, empty chairs symbolized absence and death.

Van Gogh painted no portraits of Paul Gauguin, but he did paint the chair Gauguin used during his visit. Van Gogh also made a painting of his own chair as a mate to the painting of Gauguin's. The chairs face in opposing directions, each one viewed from above. In *Gauguin's Chair*, the green and yellow of its striped seat unite the curved and spreading lines with the blurred patterns of the carpet. *Van Gogh's Chair* has lines as straight as the edge of the door behind it, and it is as rustic as the pattern of the simple floor tiles. Van Gogh said

GAUGUIN'S CHAIR

Van Gogh had an instinct for making objects fit into the environment. He linked Gauguin's chair to the carpet pattern by changing the rush seat from its natural yellow colour to green.

28

that *Gauguin's Chair* included two novels and a lighted torch 'in the absent one's place'. Perhaps the 'torch' — actually a candle — was lighting the way for Gauguin's return. A lighted candle is also an ancient symbol of life and resurrection. The gas lamp on the wall glows, creating rich bluish-purple shadows on the opposite side of the chair and making it clear that this is a night scene. One of the chair's legs extends beyond the bottom edge of the canvas.

Van Gogh's Chair was painted in daylight and takes up just about as much space as the painting of Gauguin's chair. Van Gogh's pipe and an open package of tobacco are part of the still life. Stored on the red tile floor are onions in a wooden box. Van Gogh shows a corner of it, a space just large enough for his signature. This close-up painting of his chair seems to express the feelings of comfort and rest he derived from the sturdy, simple furniture he owned in Arles.

VAN GOGH'S CHAIR
(THE CHAIR AND THE PIPE)

Van Gogh connected his chair to the room by making the thin yellow line on the door touch the top of one of the chair legs. He also repeated the pattern where the sections of the seat come together at the intersections of the floor tiles.

29

L'Arlésienne

A Fast Masterpiece

With the fields dormant, van Gogh turned to portraits during the winter months. He painted about forty, all of local people, including Madame Ginoux, who, with her husband, ran a café near his house. Madame Ginoux posed for van Gogh and Gauguin at about the same time. Gauguin painted the dignified woman's face from the front, while van Gogh preferred to pose her turned a little away from him so he could see the broad band of her headdress trailing to the back of the chair. Probably at the artist's request, Madame Ginoux dressed in a traditional costume of Arles, and hence today the painting is called *L'Arlésienne*, or 'the woman of Arles'. She was van Gogh's friend, and he had known her long enough to realize that sitting for the painting made her nervous. He obliged her by 'slashing on' the paint in less than an hour.

'Black, black, black, with perfectly raw Prussian blue,' was van Gogh's description of the colour of his model's costume. The green table on which Madame Ginoux leans is very dark, too. These deep tones in front of the lemon yellow wall make her stand out like a raven against the sun. The pages of the book and the collar of Madame Ginoux's dress are mint green. Van Gogh avoided white because it would have been too bright against the dark colours.

Exaggerated Shapes

The scalloped silhouette of Madame Ginoux's headdress delighted van Gogh, and he found similar contours in the profile of her sleeves. The shape of the arm of the chair, only partly shown, is echoed in the yellow space under Madame Ginoux's right arm. Her face is brought to life with dabs of red on her eyelids and lips. The same red outlines parts of her hand and defines the pretty embroidery on her long collar. The orange that van Gogh used to paint one of the books in front of Madame Ginoux is repeated in the chair back. The books are not just props. They elevate the portrait from one of a woman at rest to one of an intelligent reader musing over the pages before her.

Only months after van Gogh painted Madame Ginoux's portrait, he became ill. In a fit of depression, he sliced off his earlobe. Convinced that van Gogh was dangerous, Gauguin returned to Paris, and many of the people of Arles turned their backs on him as well. Fearing he was going mad, van Gogh entered a mental hospital. He was never to enjoy life in his own house again.

Van Gogh found landscapes and still lifes easier to paint than figures. But he believed that the public would be won over to modern art through portraits, so he worked hard to compose them in unusual and interesting ways.

Cypresses

Flames of Green

Van Gogh's new home was an asylum in an old priory in the mountain foothills outside the town of Saint-Rémy. He described the place as a 'rest home' and assured his brother, 'I'm all right here. . . . The fear of madness has largely fallen from me now that I see around me those afflicted with it.' He had spells when he could not paint, yet still he managed to complete more than one hundred magnificent canvases and one hundred drawings during his year-long stay in hospital.

The countryside around Saint-Rémy was more rugged than the flat plains of Arles, and van Gogh was particularly drawn to the cypress trees that abounded there. They reminded him of Egyptian obelisks in their fine proportions and beauty. They 'are always occupying my thoughts,' he wrote. 'I would like to make something of them like the canvases of the sunflowers, because it astonishes me that they have not been done as I see them.' But after he tried, he complained that he had not been able 'to do them as I feel them'. He did not give up, and in his painting *Cypresses*, he was finally able to express the strong emotion that gripped him when confronting nature.

The cypress has many small, dark evergreen needles that grow close together. Van Gogh described the colour as a 'difficult bottle-green hue'. In his painting, the trees are tinged with a yellowish green, and lavender and blue limbs show through the blanket of needles. Van Gogh applied the paint with curving and spiralling brushstrokes. The luscious strokes of colour are so thick that there are ridges and valleys everywhere on the surface of the canvas. This thickly applied paint forms a landscape of its own when viewed close up.

Van Gogh often painted two cypress trees so close together that they seem to grow out of a single trunk. Here, shrubs mask the base of the smaller tree. Van Gogh painted the taller cypress rising beyond the top of the canvas, which makes it seem even larger than it is. Twisting and turning, the trees are shaped like great flames, and the ground, the mountains and the brambles below echo their spiralling play. Dots and dashes of paint scurry through the sky, which is filled with tumbling pink clouds and a thin crescent moon. It is impossible to find a straight line anywhere in the painting.

Swirls Everywhere

Van Gogh used drawings in a number of ways. When he was learning the appearance of a place

Van Gogh covers this painting with swirling patterns. The twisting marks of his brush endow the work with rhythm and energy.

In van Gogh's pen drawings, light is represented by the paper itself, so he always had to plan where not to put ink. The darkest areas are where he placed thick lines closest together. To avoid mistakes, he usually drew the scene in pencil first.

or object, drawing was his aid. He also drew pictures in letters to his family and friends to show them what he was painting. Other drawings were copies of his paintings, which he would either keep as records or give away. He made drawings, too, as works of art in themselves, not as preparations for paintings or records to keep. It was less expensive to make a drawing than a painting, because the materials were cheaper. His reed pen, like the ones Japanese artists used, fitted into his shirt pocket, and he could carry his ink and drawing pad in one hand.

In van Gogh's drawing of the pair of cypress trees, he invented two ways of filling his landscape with motion. He formed his trees entirely of swirls, and the brambles and mountains are all heaving, curving lines. In the painting, he simplified these two designs into the one swirling pattern that fills the canvas. Just as he learned to make patterns with dots and dashes when he lived in Paris, he now turned what he saw into swirls. By filling heaven and earth with such animated and colourful energy, van Gogh found a unique way to express his awe at the fullness of creation.

WHEATFIELD

The Starry Night

To paint or draw a subject, van Gogh had to have it right in front of him. Gauguin encouraged him to compose paintings from his imagination, but he found that very difficult. Even when he was confined to his room in the hospital at Saint-Rémy, he painted what he could see from the window. He seems never to have been bored with the restricted view of the landscape he could glimpse through his window and its iron bars. There was a sloping field, an enclosing wall, three farm buildings that van Gogh could see only partially, and a mountain ridge beyond. He captured every detail of this scene in rain and shine.

Van Gogh's way of painting suddenly changed, at least for the moment. A religious subject came to his mind and he felt compelled to paint it. At last, he had an idea in his mind's eye that he could transfer to paper and canvas. The result was *The Starry Night*. He never described it in his letters or said what the subject was about, so the inner meaning of the painting is personal and secret.

The painting shows a sky alive with eleven magnified stars, each circled by dashes of silvery paint. A nebula or a comet sweeps in like a dragon, looping round the stars and curling round a second, smaller nebula. These two speeding spirals are separated from the mountaintops beneath them by a long stream of mysterious yellow light. The brightest object in the firmament is the sun, eclipsed by an orange moon. Van Gogh weds the moon and sun into one. The ribbon of mountains below this mysterious heaven shelters fields and a town. Two cypress trees, painted with brown outlines, rise up on the left, their tendrils corkscrewing towards the highest star.

Reaching for the Heavens

As van Gogh painted the picture, the sky was the most important part in his mind. He might have been recalling the Old Testament story of Joseph, who saw eleven stars and the sun and moon bowing down to him, a tale the artist knew well. The village is typically Dutch, but the landscape is the familiar one around Saint-Rémy. Like the trees, the spire of the church reaches for the heavens.

Many people consider this to be van Gogh's finest painting, even though its meaning is elusive. The subject is unique, but the reason for the painting's fame is its emotional intensity. Painted in a high pitch of religious fervour, it is a passionately spiritual work of art.

OVERLEAF:
While spinning stars and swirling comets transfigure the sky, no one seems to be present to witness the strange occurrence. Lighted windows indicate that the villagers are indoors. Van Gogh painted their houses and the church with rigid, angular lines that contrast with the flowing curves above.

First Steps, after Millet

Van Gogh's Hero

While van Gogh was in the hospital, he decided to make painted copies of Jean François Millet's prints. Millet was his idol. Born poor in rural France thirty-nine years before van Gogh, this famous artist painted peasants most of his life. When van Gogh first saw a large exhibition of drawings by Millet in Paris, he was deeply inspired. In a letter to Theo, he wrote that he should have said to himself, 'Take off your shoes, for the place where you are standing is Holy Ground.' His opinion of the man never changed; to him, Millet was 'the greatest of the greats'. Van Gogh always tried to emulate the 'truth and simplicity' of this artist's work, and even called him 'Father Millet'.

Black-and-white prints of Millet's paintings were popular during van Gogh's lifetime. Van Gogh owned a few dozen of them, and had photographs of Millet's works as well. He valued these images greatly because he felt that the

Jean François Millet
FIRST STEPS

human soul — which he called 'a precious pearl' — was visible in Millet's art. Van Gogh learned to draw people by copying figures from the prints, making them into large sketches.

Adding Colour

Transferring the peasant subjects from prints to canvas was comforting, and van Gogh completed more than a dozen such paintings. He let each print 'pose . . . as a subject', as if the printed piece of paper were a person or a vase of flowers. By making these paintings, van Gogh felt he was helping Millet, who had died almost five years before and so had 'had no time to paint [these] in oil'. Using a traditional method called scoring to copy the prints on to canvas, van Gogh made fairly exact versions of Millet's designs. First, he drew a grid of squares, on a print and on a canvas. Each had the same number of squares. It was much easier and more accurate to copy the part of the image that was in each small square one at a time on to the canvas than to copy the whole painting at once. The copying was done in pencil. Painting in the colours was the last task, and it gave van Gogh great joy. 'My brush goes between my fingers as a bow would on the violin, and absolutely for my own pleasure,' he wrote. The paintings were so different from the original black-and-white prints that the artist concluded that his task was 'much more translating them into another tongue than copying them'.

First Steps

Van Gogh's brother Theo married 'a good Dutch girl' who was called Jo. Soon she was expecting a child. As a gift to them, van Gogh decided to copy a charming scene of a young family by Millet called *First Steps*. 'How beautiful that Millet is,' he exclaimed upon seeing the photograph of it he had ordered. He scored it, copied it on to canvas with pencil, and then began enhancing it with colours that were new and unusual for him — soft, creamy greens, sun-washed yellows, whites and blues.

What was not unusual for van Gogh was the way he put on the paint. For trees and bushes, he twisted his brush to make spirals. Small, wavy motions of his hand produced the earth of the vegetable garden and the thatched roofs of the farm buildings. Darker lines around the edges of the three figures made them stand out. The outlines of the wheelbarrow were filled in with

touches of tan and green paint. Van Gogh sent
his painting to his brother and sister-in-law as
soon as it was dry. A son was born on 31 January
1890, and they named him Vincent Willem.
When van Gogh's stay in the Saint-Rémy asylum
was over, he hurried to Paris to see his namesake.

Van Gogh selected pastel colours because he thought this painting
might hang in the new baby's nursery. In his letters, van Gogh
mentioned Millet more than any other artist, admiring Millet's ability
to picture humble peasants as noble human beings.

Crows over a Wheatfield

Van Gogh liked his sister-in-law and was happy to be in the midst of the new family. He was also able to visit Père Tanguy and other old friends.

Just an hour's journey outside Paris, on the river Oise, was the quiet town of Auvers, where he decided to live. Going to bed at nine most nights, and rising at five to ensure a full day's light for painting, van Gogh led a disciplined life. He completed about one canvas a day. This speed, he explained, was 'to express the desperately rapid passing of things in modern life'. The thatched cottages of Auvers, falling into ruin, were just such 'things', so he painted them to record their appearance before they were gone forever. The modern villas, the church, the fields and farms were other subjects. He also found interesting people to paint.

Above Auvers was a seemingly endless plateau of wheatfields spreading to the horizon. Van Gogh wanted to capture the vastness of the scene, so he chose a canvas twice as wide as it was tall. When he got to the site, a storm was brewing and he saw a fast-changing scene in front of him. In his painting, black crows hurry to find shelter.

Van Gogh's boldly painted expanses of blue and gold converge with stripes of red and green. The large marks of his brush bring these four regions of colour together into a restless composition.

45

The sun shines above the wheat, making it glow like gold as the wind bends it to the ground. Echoing the shapes of the crows, strokes of deep red make wavelike marks across the ocean of wheat to show how it ripples. To paint the scene, van Gogh stood at the junction of three lanes cut into the field by farm carts to plant and harvest. He drew attention to the red-clay colour of the dusty lanes by painting margins of weeds on either side of them in bright green, their complementary colour. The long, wavy lines he used to show the weeds and the lanes seem to flow like rivers towards the bottom of the canvas, where they join into one road.

Van Gogh painted a number of views of the wheatfields above Auvers and was eager to show them to Theo. He wrote to his brother that he saw 'health and restorative forces' in the countryside. While the storm in *Crows over a Wheatfield* appears to some viewers as an omen of van Gogh's death, he himself saw the golden wheat as an affirmation of life.

A Final Home

Two months after he moved to Auvers, van Gogh shot himself with a pistol. He died two days later, on 29 July 1890. Why Vincent van Gogh committed suicide will never be known, but the day before he died, his brother Theo, who had hurried from Paris to be at his side, said, 'He feels so alone.' It is not certain which of van Gogh's works was the last one he painted, but *Crows over a Wheatfield* was completed in the days just before his death.

Van Gogh was buried in a new cemetery on the edge of the wheatfields. Theo died six months later, and was buried next to his brother. His widow, Jo, took care of van Gogh's paintings and saved the hundreds of letters he had sent to Theo. She taught her son to honour his uncle as the greatest artist who ever lived. When Vincent Willem was an old man, he helped to start the Vincent van Gogh Museum in Amsterdam. All of Vincent's paintings and drawings that Theo had accumulated during Vincent's brief life — and that Theo, Jo and Vincent Willem had lovingly preserved — were passed on to the museum. It was van Gogh's gift to the people of the world.

IRISES

What Makes a van Gogh

Van Gogh's paintings are filled with bold colour and vivid patterns.

1.

4.

2.

3.

5.

1. He placed complementary colours next to one another to increase their effect.

2. He laid down thick layers of paint.

3. Van Gogh created shadows and reflections with a combination of colours, not just with black.

4. His brushstrokes are vigorous and form strong patterns.

5. Van Gogh outlined his figures to make them stand out against the background.

a van Gogh?

THE BANK OF THE OISE AT AUVERS

Index